Festive Foods for the Holidays™

A Thanksgiving Holiday COOKBOOK

Emily Raabe

The Rosen Publishing Group's
PowerKids Press™
New York

The recipes in this cookbook
are intended for a child to make together with an adult.

Many thanks to Ruth Rosen and her test kitchen

For Rachel, my favorite chef

Published in 2002 by The Rosen Publishing Group, Inc.
29 East 21st Street, New York, NY 10010

Copyright © 2002 by The Rosen Publishing Group, Inc.

First Edition

Book Design: Maria E. Melendez
Project Editor: Frances E. Ruffin

Photo Credits: Cover and title page, pp. 10 (Pilgrims), 14 (first Thanksgiving), 18, 20 © Bettmann/CORBIS; pp. 4, 10, 16 © SuperStock; p. 9 © John Michael/International Stock; p. 13 © North Wind Picture Archives; Ingredients on cover, title page, and recipe pages © Digital Stock; All recipe photos by Arlan Dean; Page number designs created by Maria E. Melendez.

Raabe, Emily.
A Thanksgiving holiday cookbook / Emily Raabe.
    p. cm. — (Festive foods for the holidays)
Includes bibliographical references and index.
  ISBN 0–8239–5628–8 (library binding)
1. Thanksgiving cookery—Juvenile literature. 2. Thanksgiving Day—History—Juvenile literature. [1. Thanksgiving Day—History. 2. Thanksgiving cookery.
3. Cookery, American. 4. Holidays.] I. Title. II. Series.
  TX739.2.T45 R33 2002
  641.5'68—dc21
                                                                                                    2001000253

Manufactured in the United States of America

Contents

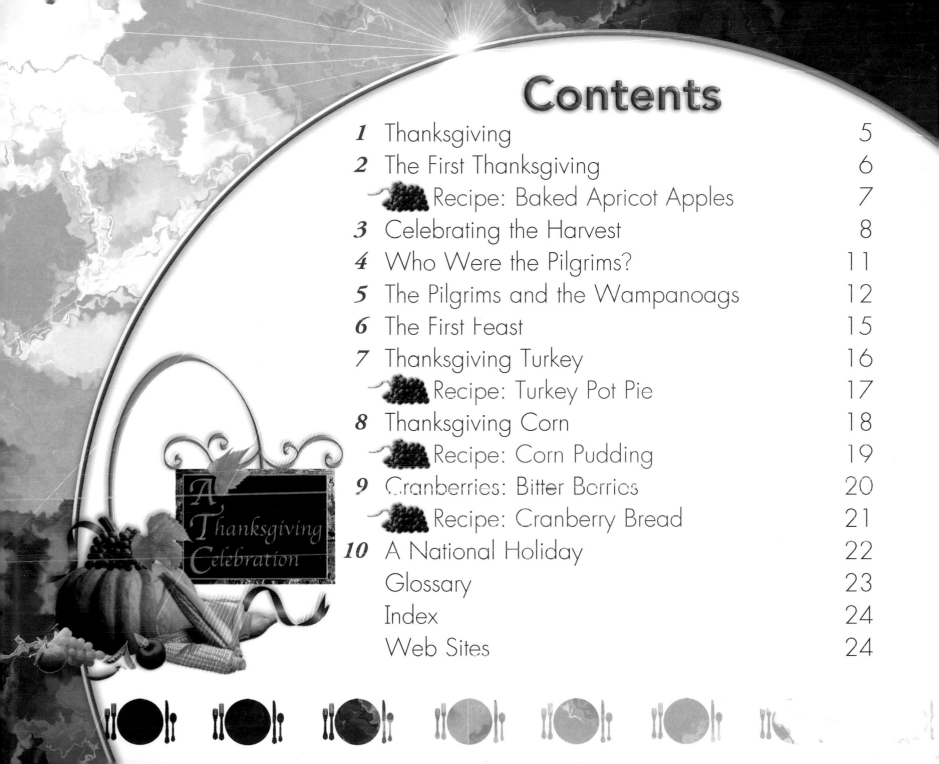

A Thanksgiving Celebration

Thanksgiving

Every year, on the fourth Thursday in November, Americans **celebrate** Thanksgiving. It is a time for giving thanks for the **blessings** of the past year, and for sharing a big meal with family and friends. For most Americans, a Thanksgiving dinner usually includes roast turkey and stuffing made with breadcrumbs. The Thanksgiving table also might hold yams or sweet potatoes, peas, green beans, squash, turnips, cranberry sauce, nuts, fruits, and desserts, such as pumpkin or apple pies. People enjoy and include **regional** foods in different parts of the country. In North Carolina, you might add oysters to your Thanksgiving dinner. In Oregon, you might add salmon. Americans have been celebrating Thanksgiving for almost 500 years.

Many people eat their Thanksgiving dinner in the afternoon, rather than at night. After the meal, they might play a game or go for a walk, or just sit and rest after eating all that food!

The First Thanksgiving

Thanksgiving began with a three-day feast that took place in 1621. The people who ate that first feast were Pilgrims from England who had settled in Plymouth, Massachusetts. The Pilgrims shared their feast with the Wampanoags, the Native Americans who lived in the area. Some of the foods that we eat today during Thanksgiving also were eaten by the Pilgrims and the Wampanoags. Other foods have been added over the years to the **traditional** Thanksgiving feast. The Pilgrims and the Wampanoags enjoyed fruits, such as grapes, dried plums, and many kinds of berries. Today apples are a favorite fruit served at Thanksgiving. Here is a delicious and an easy-to-make recipe for baked apples with apricot preserves.

Baked Apricot Apples

You will need:

8 baking apples, cored
¾ cup (177 ml) of apricot preserves
¼ teaspoon (1.2 ml) ground ginger
¼ teaspoon (1.2 ml) ground coriander
1 teaspoon (5 ml) ground cinnamon

How to do it:

Preheat the oven to 375 degrees Fahrenheit (191 °C).

Mix apricot preserves with the spices. Spoon mixture into the apples.

Place apples in a baking dish. Add ½ inch (1.3 cm) of water.

Bake for 45–60 minutes, basting often with the water (this means spooning the water over the apples).

Serves 8.

Celebrating the Harvest

The first Thanksgiving was actually not a Thanksgiving at all! The Pilgrims' feast was really a harvest celebration. It probably was very similar to the harvest feasts that they had celebrated at home in England. In 1622, the second year that the Pilgrims lived in Plymouth, there were more **settlers** from England to feed, and less food. There was no harvest feast at all that year. The third year in Plymouth, there was a **drought**. The crops could not grow without rain, and the settlers began to starve. The governor of Plymouth, William Bradford, ordered a day of fasting and praying. Soon after that, the rains came. Governor Bradford made June 30, 1623, a day of celebration.

People around the world always have held celebrations at harvesttime. In America, pumpkins, squashes, Indian corn, and fall flowers appear around harvesttime.

8

The Pilgrims and the Wampanoags

After sailing for 66 days, the Pilgrims arrived at what is now the state of Massachusetts. The Pilgrims named their new home Plymouth, after the place they had left in England. During the first winter in Plymouth, the settlers did not have enough food to eat. Many became sick and half of them died. All might have died if they had not been helped by the Wampanoag natives who lived near Plymouth. A Native American named Squanto showed the Pilgrims how to fish and plant corn. He told them which berries and wild plants to eat. Without Squanto's help, the Pilgrims never would have survived in America.

This is an illustration of a Wampanoag man. The Wampanoag people lived all over what is now southeastern Massachusetts and Rhode Island. Their name means "eastern people."

The First Feast

After the first hard winter, things got better for the Pilgrims. By October 1621, the settlers had corn, beans, peas, squashes, berries, fish, venison, which is deer meat, and wild turkey to eat. The governor of Plymouth, William Bradford, decided it was a good time to give thanks for their harvest and for **surviving** a difficult winter. The Pilgrims invited their Native American neighbors to come to a feast. Ninety-one Wampanoags came to the feast. They hunted for five deer and shared the venison with the settlers. The Pilgrims and the Wampanoags ate, played games, ran races, sang, and danced together. Today Thanksgiving lasts for only one day. The settlers' feast lasted for three days!

The settlers and Indians probably roasted their venison over an open fire and ate their turkey roasted or boiled. They had no forks, only fingers, spoons, and knives with which to eat their food.

15

Thanksgiving Turkey

The Pilgrims had a lot of meat and fish in their diets. They probably ate roast goose, venison, and duck, and enjoyed lobster and fish at their harvest feast. For vegetables, they probably had stewed pumpkin and puddings made from corn. One familiar food at the Pilgrims' feast was turkey. The Pilgrims found wild turkeys in the area, which they caught and ate.

This painting shows Pilgrims chasing after wild turkeys.

Today most Thanksgiving dinners include turkey. After Thanksgiving, people enjoy eating turkey sandwiches and delicious dishes made from leftover turkey. This turkey pot pie recipe is a great way for you to enjoy your leftover Thanksgiving turkey.

16

Turkey Pot Pie

You will need:

1 can, 10 oz (284 g), cream of mushroom soup

1 cup (237 ml) milk

1 cup (237 ml) canned or frozen peas

1 pimento, sliced

1½ cups (355 ml) cooked turkey, cubed

1 box, 6 oz (170 g), cornbread stuffing

How to do it:

Preheat the oven to 375 degrees Fahrenheit (191 °C).

Combine the soup and milk in a saucepan over medium heat.

Add the peas, pimento, and turkey, and stir.

Heat mixture, stirring, for 1 minute.

Pour mixture into a shallow baking dish.

Prepare the cornbread stuffing mix according to the package directions.

Spoon the stuffing over the turkey, pea, and pimento mixture.

Bake in the oven for 25 to 30 minutes, until bubbling.

Serves 4.

Thanksgiving Corn

Corn is a popular Thanksgiving **symbol**. This is because corn was one of the Pilgrims' most important foods. The Pilgrims planted and ate Indian corn. Indian corn is small and colored red, yellow, black, green, or blue. Squanto showed the Pilgrims how to plant corn under mounds of dirt. He also told them to bury dead fish in the mounds. As the fish rotted, they added **nutrients** to the soil. The Pilgrims dried the corn and then pounded it into cornmeal to use for cornbreads and corn puddings. This corn pudding recipe is similar to a corn pudding that the Pilgrims might have eaten at their feast.

18

Corn Pudding

You will need:

2 eggs

2 tablespoons (30 ml) sugar

2 tablespoons (30 ml) cornstarch

1 can cream-style corn

1 can, 14 oz (398 ml), evaporated milk

2 tablespoons (30 ml) melted butter

How to do it:

Preheat the oven to 325 Fahrenheit (163 °C).

In a large bowl, beat the eggs.

Add the sugar, cornstarch, corn, milk, and butter.

Stir until blended.

Pour into a greased, oven-safe dish.

Bake for 1 hour.

Serves 4.

Cranberries: Bitter Berries

Like corn and turkey, cranberries were an important food for the Pilgrims and for the Wampanoags. Cranberries grew in cranberry **bogs** all around Plymouth. Squanto and other Native Americans showed the settlers the berries that they called *ibimi*, meaning "bitter berry." Cranberries are an important source of vitamin C, the vitamin that prevents a disease called **scurvy**. Whenever settlers had to travel back to England, they always took cranberries on the trip with them to keep from getting sick. The Wampanoags mixed cranberries with dried venison to make a flat cake called pemmican. Today, at Thanksgiving, people eat cranberry sauces and pies. This cranberry bread is a sweet and delicious way to enjoy cranberries.

Cranberry Bread

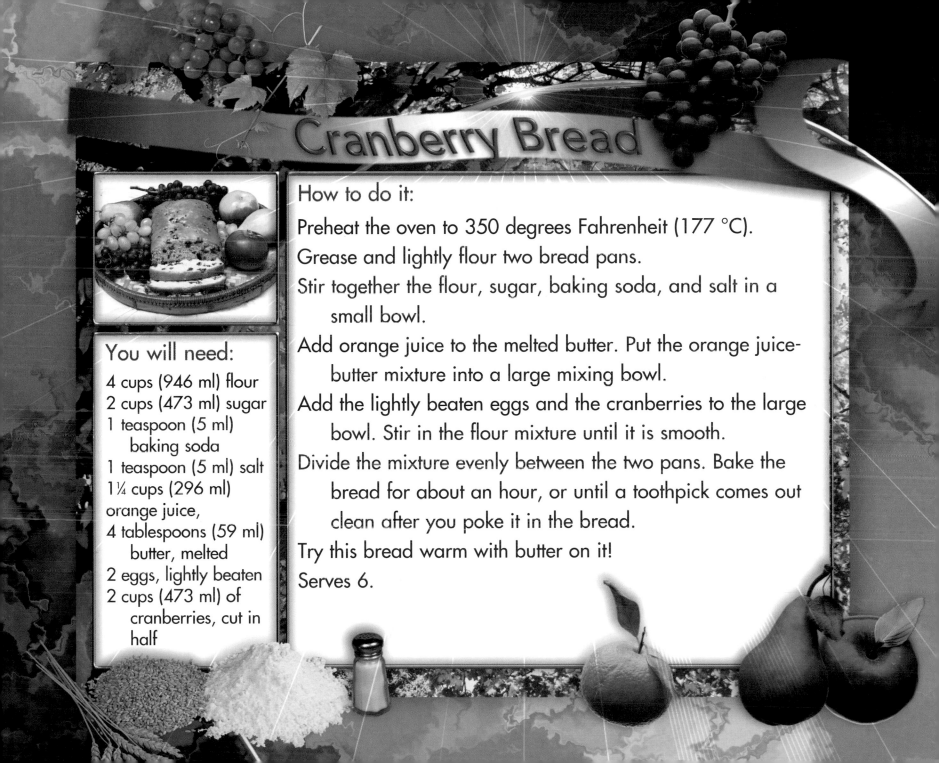

You will need:

4 cups (946 ml) flour
2 cups (473 ml) sugar
1 teaspoon (5 ml) baking soda
1 teaspoon (5 ml) salt
1¼ cups (296 ml) orange juice,
4 tablespoons (59 ml) butter, melted
2 eggs, lightly beaten
2 cups (473 ml) of cranberries, cut in half

How to do it:

Preheat the oven to 350 degrees Fahrenheit (177 °C).

Grease and lightly flour two bread pans.

Stir together the flour, sugar, baking soda, and salt in a small bowl.

Add orange juice to the melted butter. Put the orange juice-butter mixture into a large mixing bowl.

Add the lightly beaten eggs and the cranberries to the large bowl. Stir in the flour mixture until it is smooth.

Divide the mixture evenly between the two pans. Bake the bread for about an hour, or until a toothpick comes out clean after you poke it in the bread.

Try this bread warm with butter on it!

Serves 6.

A National Holiday

For many years after the first Thanksgiving, days of thanksgiving were celebrated for a good harvest, a victory in a battle, or a time of good living. George Washington ordered a national day of thanksgiving on November 26, 1789. At the end of the **Civil War**, in 1865, President Abraham Lincoln made the last Thursday in November a similar holiday for the entire nation. Today Thanksgiving is still a time to give thanks for good food and happiness, just as it was for the Pilgrims in 1621. It is the perfect time to cook delicious food to share with your family and your friends!

Glossary

blessings (BLEH-sings) Prayers of thanks to God.

bogs (BOGZ) Places where the ground is wet and marshy.

celebrate (SEH-luh-brayt) To observe a special time or day with festive activities.

Civil War (SIH-vul WOR) The war fought between the northern and southern states of America from 1861 to 1865.

drought (DROWT) A long period of dry weather with little or no rain.

hardtack (HARD-tak) A hard biscuit made without salt.

nutrients (NOO-tree-ints) Anything that a living thing needs for life and growth.

regional (REE-jeh-nuhl) Referring to different parts of a country.

scurvy (SKUR-vee) A disease that is caused by a lack of vitamin C.

settlers (SET-lerz) People who move to a new land.

surviving (sur-VYV-ing) Staying alive.

symbol (SIM-bul) An object or a design that stands for something important.

traditional (truh-DISH-nul) A way of doing something that is passed down through the years.

23

Index

Web Sites

For more Information about Thanksgiving and the Pilgrims, check out these Web sites:

www.plimoth.org/Library/Thanksgiving/firstT.htm

www.pilgrimhall.org/thanksg.htm

24